Paula Breslich

Indoor Plants

Albany Books

Designed and produced by
Albany Books
36 Park Street London W1Y 4DE

First published 1978

Published by Albany Books

Printed in Hong Kong

The publishers acknowledge permission
to reproduce photographs from the
following owners: William MacQuitty;
Natural Science Photographs (N. H.
Agnew, I. Bennett, P. A. Bowman,
E. Crichton, G. Montalverne); Harry
Smith Horticultural Photographic
Collection; Spectrum Colour Library;
Peter Stiles.

Introduction

It is not difficult to have success with houseplants—even for inexperienced plant enthusiasts—but it is very important to marshall the facts and find out just what conditions suit your plants best. Far too often out of ignorance plants are allowed to languish through over- or under-watering, too much or too little sunlight or simply lack of care in keeping the leaves clean, repotting when necessary or feeding properly. The object of this book is to set out as clearly as possible the ideal conditions for a wide number of popular houseplants and the dangers to watch out for.

Plant Adaptability

It is only common sense to try to create an environment for your plant as similar as possible to its original habitat in heat, light, moisture and humidity. Obviously a cactus should be watered sparingly and given as much light as possible, whereas a tropical plant like the Prayer Plant (*Maranta*) needs a high degree of humidity, heat and moisture. However, most fortunately for the indoor plant enthusiast, plants are surprisingly adaptable.

Not unlike some human beings plants dislike sudden change, and this is often the reason for a plant's demise soon after being purchased. In the winter, if the plant is not sufficiently protected, the journey between nursery and house might be enough to spell doom for it. A good rule of thumb is to make changes gradually. If you purchase a plant which has been kept for some time in less than ideal conditions it is better to recreate these conditions for a time, giving the plant a chance to adapt, rather than to plunge it suddenly into opposite conditions. Then you you can slowly make changes which will mean a healthier plant in future.

Light

Most plants need a fair amount of light but there are some which cannot bear direct sunlight. Equally, some plants (like ferns) prefer shade or at least will tolerate shade, and these can brighten up the dark corners of your house. Artificial light is also important as it will affect the annual rhythm of your plants, and night lighting should be taken into account when considering the amount of light necessary for your plants.

Humidity and Moisture

The correct amount of moisture for your plants is one of the easiest things to provide but, in contrast, enough humidity can be one of the most difficult. Some plants which receive a high amount of humidity in their natural environment can adjust to less as is the case with the Cheese Plant (*Monstera*) which needs surprisingly little. But others still need humid conditions and unless you have installed a humidifier, central heating can make this difficult. There are some remedies such as placing the pot into or on a bed of damp peat, or using a large bowl of water in a plant display. And you must keep the plant away from any direct source of heat. However, if your house is generally quite dry and you haven't the time or inclination to work at providing a more humid atmosphere it would be best to stick to hardier plants and avoid disappointment.

Over- and under-watering are two major causes of unhealthy plants. The symptoms of both are the same—leaves turning brown, lower leaves falling off—but commonsense will tell you which it is. A plant which has dried out should be given a thorough soak immediately but not left sitting in water, and an over-watered plant should be allowed to dry out completely and should then be watered again with great care. If you water directly into the pot, stop when the water has penetrated through to the roots. A more satisfactory method of watering is allowing the roots to take up water from below. Stand your plant in a shallow dish and support it with pebbles. Pour water into the dish allowing it to be absorbed and topping up with water so that the soil on top remains moist (*not* wet). This method is useful for African Violets as it reduces the possibility

of mould to which they are particularly prone.

The amount of water needed will vary with the temperature and humidity of the surroundings. Plants—especially those with a dormant phase—will need less water in winter and more in summer.

Temperature

In general plants need a lower temperature at night and higher during the day which is the case anyway in most homes. It is important to maintain the correct minimum or maximum temperature, however, so if you live in a particularly cold climate and the house is unheated at night make sure that plants placed in windows can withstand the colder temperature. Equally, if your house is heated at night find a cool spot for plants which require a lower temperature.

Pots and Re-potting

Good drainage is of the utmost importance so do not bother potting into an attractive bowl which will not allow drainage. Old-fashioned earthenware pots are very nice and the material is porous allowing the roots to "breathe". However, plastic pots are more prevalent nowadays and are perfectly adequate though not nearly so attractive. Small stones or pieces of crockery placed in the bottom of the pot will also help with drainage.

There are two main reasons for re-potting: a larger pot may be needed to accommodate the plant roots, or a change of soil may be needed. Some plants do well being "pot-bound" as this cuts back root growth and seems to encourage flowering. Some foliage plants also do not mind being pot-bound. However, in general when your pot becomes a mass of roots this means

9

a larger pot is needed. Choose a pot only slightly larger than the one you have as the soil in a too-large pot may go sour without root activity.

Sometimes if a plant has exhausted the nutritive elements in its soil or if the pot has become moulded or discoloured in some way (for example, after long periods of feeding with liquid fertilizers), the plant will need transferring to another pot of the same size. The soil must be moist but not wet so that it comes out of the pot easily. Shake the soil free from the roots taking care not to damage them, and re-pot in new soil.

Pests and Diseases

The pests most likely to attack your plants are aphis (aphids), white fly, mealy bug, thrips, scale insects and red spider mite. There are many good insecticides available to combat these pests which must be treated immediately. Red spider mite is one of the most dangerous because it is so difficult to detect in its early stages. Insecticide sprays are convenient and not messy, but much more effective is plunging the plant leaves, not roots, into the insecticide so that the entire surface area of the plant is covered.

Fungus and mildew on leaves can be treated with a fungicide and the infected parts of roots can be cut out. However, virus diseases (fortunately rare, mainly attacking orchids) are always fatal and the infected plant and anything it has come into contact which must be destroyed. Symptoms are discolouration of the leaves by rings of dead cells and deformed growth.

Keeping Your Plants Clean

Even the toughest and most durable foliage plant will begin to look shabby and uncared for without regular cleaning. There are many of these long-suffering plants in hotels and offices the world over. Careful cleaning of the leaves with a milk-water solution will not only give the plant a much brighter appearance but will keep it healthy as plants need to breathe through their foliage. Dirt or smog collecting on the leaves will interfere with this function. There are commercial preparations which you can apply to keep the leaves shiny.

Propagation of Existing Plants

In the following list of plants methods of propagation are only mentioned where the plant can be easily propagated. Some cuttings from softwood plants take root with almost ridiculous ease at room temperature while cuttings from certain tropical plants require constant temperatures around 25°C (77°F) to root successfully (which is impractical without a special, heated propagator). In many other cases, however, you can improvise by covering your cutting with clear plastic, which will maintain the necessary humidity content. If you do this remember to "air" the cuttings twice a day for about ten minutes to counteract mould to which they are particularly susceptible.

Cuttings

Take a two- to three-inch cutting by slicing cleanly just below a node and gently removing the leaves of the bottom node. Placed in water, cuttings from softwood plants such as the geranium or Busy Lizzie (*Impatiens*) will take root easily. Leaf cuttings (leaves with stems attached) from African Violets also root easily in water. When a good

12

set of roots has grown, plant into small pots. Alternatively, place leaf or stem cuttings into a rooting mixture, and when they are growing well transplant them into small pots with a proper potting mixture. If cuttings are reluctant to root, try dipping the cut end into a hormone rooting powder. Generally speaking, the best time to take cuttings is in the spring, although for leaf cuttings you must wait until the leaves are well formed.

Root and Bulb Division

Plants which form clumps can be propagated quite simply by carefully dividing the roots and re-potting. If the roots are especially close together you may have to slice through them, but if you do, sprinkle the cut surface with a fungicide powder as a precaution against rot.

Some bulbs can be divided when they have started to sprout. Making sure that there is a shoot on both sides cut down the middle, sprinkle cut surfaces with fungicide and re-pot. Tuberous *Begonias* can be divided this way.

How this book is organized

The list of plants is divided into two sections: 1–Flowering or Fruit-bearing Plants, and 2–Foliage Plants. Plants which bear flowers of little significance are included in "Foliage Plants" rather than the first section, since they are chiefly valued for their leaves. The plants themselves are listed alphabetically by their botanical names rather than their popular names because each plant often has three or four different common names, making for vast confusion in identification. However, an exhaustive index of popular names is included with a cross-reference to their more precise botanical names.

The illustration of each plant appears next to the entry unless otherwise indicated in italics at the end of the entry.

1 Flowering and Fruitbearing Plants

Abutilon striatum thompsonii

Flowering Maple
Chinese Bellflower
Indiana Maple

This is one of the most attractive and also most readily available of the abutilons. It has the typical "maple" leaves—dark green with yellow mottling—and bell-shaped, salmon-orange flowers. Propagate in spring from seed or cutting. It needs plenty of light to flower, a temperature of around 20°C (68°F) and a lot of water when active, although it must never be stood in water. With proper light and warmth it may blossom throughout winter.

Acalypha hispida

Red-hot Cat's Tail
Chenille Plant

The main attraction of this plant is the pendulous, beetroot-red flowers that are rather like cats' tails and are freely produced in the summer. It does best in warm conditions (19°C/66°F) where the atmosphere is kept humid by frequently spraying the area around the plant or plunging the pot into damp peat. For most people, a plant to buy from the florist, enjoy for the flowering season and then throw away. Watch out for mealy bug and red spider mite.

Aechmia fasciata

Grecian Urn Plant

This unusual and dramatic houseplant may be as much as 6 centimetres (2 feet) across and 4.5 centimetres (18 inches) tall when full-grown. The leaves are grey-green and there is a beautiful stem of sharp-pointed pink bracts which enclose small, blue flowers gradually turning to pink. These colourful

bracts will last for many months. When the leaves fade and die they should be cut away to allow new shoots to take over. Although well worth keeping for its foliage, the plant is unlikely to flower again. Water freely into the centre funnel of the plant as well as the soil and spray overhead in summer, but do not over-water in winter. Keep it warm but away from strong sunlight. The bathroom often provides a favourable warm and moist atmosphere for the *Aechmia* (along with the African Violet).
Previous page

Anthurium scherzerianum

Flamingo Flower
Painter's Palette

This exotic red flower with its projecting spadix and heart-shaped leaves seems either to attract or repel people. It is wise to choose a plant in flower because the flowers will last well but are by no means easy to produce. A bright position by a window but not exposed to full sunshine and a relatively warm and humid atmosphere is best. You may propagate by division but take great care not to damage the fragile roots.
Top left

Aphelandra squarrosa louisae

Zebra Plant

The Zebra Plant, so-called because of its colourful white-veined leaves, has considerable value as a foliage plant in addition to its long-lasting yellow flowers. It should be given a lot of light and moisture until it flowers, when it will last longer if kept in a drier atmosphere (although severe drying out of the potting mixture may result in loss of leaves). New plants can be easily reared from stem cuttings inserted in sandy compost.
Left

Begonia semperflorens
Wax Begonia

This brilliant flowering begonia may easily be raised from seed to full flower in six months, and its summer to autumn flowering period is gratifyingly long. It should be thrown away after this period since it tends not to do well during a second season. It succeeds as a pot plant in a well-lit room, kept moist and shaded from direct sunlight. As with the *Begonia rex* the *semperflorens* may be afflicted by mildew.
Previous page and top left

Beloperone guttata
Shrimp Plant

Given warm, lightly shaded and moist conditions this will develop into a spectacular plant. As suggested by its common name the bracts are a pinkish colour, and they do look remarkably like shrimp. In the early stages of growth, the growing tips should be regularly pinched out and the early flowering bracts should also be removed to promote more vigorous leaf growth and a more compact plant. To keep your plant healthy feed it regularly and pot on to make room for root growth.
Bottom left

Billbergia nutans
Angel's Tears   Queen's Tears

The pendulous, tubular flowers of this plant are a curiously shaded combination of pink, yellow, blue and green. They are attractive but unfortunately short-lived and difficult to induce again. However, the plant may be kept for its leaves which are long and tough. It will tolerate considerable temperature variation although it does better in a steady temperature in the region of 19°C (66°F). Keep the soil moist but not wet.
Right

Bulbs

There are a number of bulbs which can be easily forced to flower in winter, ranging from the hyacinth with its masses of sweet-smelling flowers to delicate crocuses, irises, tulips and narcissi.

Planting Bulbs

This method of planting may be used for all hyacinths and crocuses. In the case of irises, tulips and narcissi it is important to take the advice of a reputable bulb supplier since some respond well to this indoor treatment and others not.

In the autumn cover bulbs with moist bulb fibre. Do not force the bulbs down into the fibre but pack the fibre carefully around the bulbs so that the roots will grow downwards. The tops of the hyacinths and narcissi should protrude slightly but in all other cases should be completely covered. It is very important to find a dark, cool place for them to develop. Unless you live in an exceptionally cold district you may stand them outside surrounded with black plastic and covered well with ashes, leaves or sand. After eight or nine weeks, when leaf buds begin to form, move them to an equally cool place with moderate light. (The temperature is very important as heat will cause the leaves to develop at the expense of the flowers.) As soon as flower buds are visible you should move into full light and a moderate temperature. When they are about to flower move them to a position of less light. They prefer a moist humid atmosphere. After flowering it is best to throw away bulbs used indoors as they are rarely as good the second year.

Top left: Iris. *Top right:* Narcissi. *Bottom left:* Tulip. *Centre and right:* Hyacinths

Calceolaria

Purse Flower   Slipper Flower

There is a wide range of these exotic and gaily-coloured pouch-shaped flowers. Although yellow predominates, the flowers come in a number of colours and are often splashed or speckled with a contrasting shade. Good light is necessary although they do not like brilliant sunshine or high temperatures. Keep the soil moist but not wet and watch out for green fly to which *Calceolaria* are particularly prone. They are annuals and not to be kept on after flowering.

Camellia

Camellias have the double advantage of bearing shiny, evergreen leaves as well as beautiful flowers of classical purity ranging in colour from snow white to deepest red. They will flower in autumn, winter or spring and prefer to be moved out of doors during the summer when not in flower. They will not survive well at high temperatures, so should be placed in a cool, light part of the room. Be careful not to dry out the soil or to overwater. Propagate by cuttings. *Right*

Campanula isophylla

Star of Bethlehem   Italian Bellflower

Given only a modest amount of attention this attractive and easy-to-grow trailing plant will produce lovely lilac-blue or white flowers throughout the summer. It grows well hanging from a basket or a stand or trailing down the side of a table. Unfortunately it dies back in winter when it must be kept almost wholly dry, but encourage by watering as soon as new growth starts. Otherwise it likes plenty of light and a moderate amount of watering while flowering.

Capsicum annuum

Ornamental Pepper
Christmas Pepper
Guinea Pepper
Chilli Pepper
Red Pepper

There are many varieties of the Christmas Pepper, all bearing attractive chilli fruits in many colours. They usually appear in shops at an advanced stage in their cycle with some of the fruit already ripe. To maintain the fruit they need cool, light conditions and should not be over-watered. To raise your own plants sew fresh seed in the spring, thin out the shoots and transfer to 75-millimetre (3-inch) pots as soon as possible, then pot on to 150- or 175-millimetre (6- or 7-inch) pots.

Chrysanthemum

Choose a healthy plant with a large number of unopened buds and resist the impulse to have a big splash of colour immediately. To keep the plant as long as possible, maintain a cool temperature (around 15°C/59°F if possible) and water frequently. Most plants bought in shops have been dwarfed with chemicals, so if you keep them on after flowering they may grow to a considerable height. Keep the plant slightly moist over winter and when growth begins in spring take cuttings and discard the old roots
Left

Citrus mitis

Calamondin Orange

This enchanting miniature orange bears tiny tangerine-shaped fruit and has delicately scented white flowers almost throughout the year. It will benefit from being stood outside in the summer but take care not to return it suddenly into a dry, centrally-heated atmosphere. It flourishes in a bright, moist yet airy space.

Clivia

Kaffir Lily

This plant has handsome year-round foliage as well as flamboyant, clusters of flowers. The blooms appear from spring to summer, and a temperature of only 4°C (39°F) is needed in winter. If kept constantly at a higher temperature than this it may bloom early. It makes a sturdy houseplant, thriving in half-shaded conditions, and seldom needs re-potting. Keep it moist until it blooms when you should water freely.

Above

26

Coffea arabica

Arabian Coffee Plant

Its glossy green leaves make this a lovely foliage plant and if grown to the size of a small bush it will produce masses of white, very fragrant flowers. These are followed by red berries that contain coffee beans. It likes plenty of humidity and air and a temperature around 20°C (68°F). Keep the soil moist.

Crocus See **Bulbs**

Cuphea ignea

Mexican Cigar Plant

This fast-flowering plant may produce a few flowers when only a seedling, but it will go on to become a full-grown, shrubby plant covered with scarlet, tubular-shaped flowers with black tips. It is easy to grow from seed and needs only a small pot for cultivation. Place in a light position and keep the soil moist. It withstands quite cool conditions.

Cyclamen

Alpine Violet

This graceful and popular flowering plant unfortunately epitomises the problems faced by lovers of indoor plants. It flowers in winter and at this time needs a constant, cool temperature around 15°C (68°F). It dislikes draughts and needs a high degree of moisture in the atmosphere. Great care must be taken with watering, and the best method is to immerse the pot in water three-quarters up for a few minutes. Do not water-log the plant; it requires rather dry soil coupled with a moist atmosphere to survive.
Top right

Cymbidium

Orchid

This is a magnificent plant with long spikes of large, colourful flowers, and contrary to popular belief about orchids, the plant can survive almost gross neglect. It flowers near the end of winter and early spring. It is best watered from the bottom, but don't let the pot stand in water for more than an hour. The compost should be kept moist but not soaking. It likes as much light as possible and a temperature of 20–25°C (68–77°F) when flowering.
Right

Dendrobium

Orchid

This orchid has delicately graceful, often white flowers which vary widely in form. It likes lots of light, a high temperature and humidity during the growth period (between spring and autumn), but after flowering it prefers drier and colder conditions. Shortly before the growth of new roots in spring, it should be re-planted in an open, well-drained potting mixture.

Echinocereus fitchii

Hedgehog Cactus

This is one of the easiest cacti to flower, producing manificent pink blooms up to 90 millimetres ($3\frac{1}{2}$ inches) in diameter after only two years. It begins as a solitary upright plant but branches from the base as it matures. It is better to under- rather than over-water the cactus allowing it nearly to dry out before its next watering. It should have as much light as possible during the day, and a maximum temperature of 25°C (77°F) during the active season and a minimum of 10°C (50°F) during the inactive season.
Bottom left

Erica

Heather

Heather is one of the most attractive winter flowering plants. It grows best in light conditions free from draughts and well away from hot air or any heat supply. In fact they do best if kept at a temperature below 20°C (68°F). There must also be plenty of moisture but good drainage. If the pot dries out completely the result is fatal.
Left

Euphorbia milii (syn. **E. Splendens**)

Crown of Thorns

Along with its many thorns this plant has small oval leaves and bright red flowers. Although outdoors it may grow to a vast, straggling shrub it makes a good indoor plant as it is a fairly slow grower and has the advantage of flowering when young. It prefers a light room and needs plenty of water when in growth but very little when inactive. *Above*

Fatsia japonica

Fig-leaved Palm
False Castor-oil Plant

Its large, glossy, finger-cut leaves and clusters of creamy flowers make this a particularly attractive indoor plant. A mature plant may grow to 25–30 centimetres (8–10 feet) in height, but it usually remains more compact than this. It likes cool conditions (around 13°C/55°F) and annual potting on when small. Keep the soil reasonably moist and place the plant in a shady spot in the house.
Right

Fuchsia

The strikingly handsome and long-blooming flowers of the fuchsia make this a coveted indoor plant. There are many varieties to choose from in a wide range of colours. Adequate light is essential although some sun protection will be required. Water copiously and feed during the flowering season. They prefer a cool temperature not higher than 20°C (68°F). Cuttings will root in water.
Left

Haemanthus

Blood Lily

Spectacular bunches of flowers in various shades of red, orange and white grow atop short, thickish stems making the *Haemanthus* an attractive but unusual looking plant. Bulbs are best planted in spring with their necks just above the surface of moist soil and full watering should not begin until shoots appear. The flowering plant requires plenty of light and a moist soil. It should only need re-potting every three years.
Bottom left

Heliotropium peruvianum

Heliotrope
Cherry Pie

Heliotrope is an easy houseplant and well worth having because of its lovely scented flowers. When not in growth it should be kept on the dry side, but otherwise it likes a moist soil and plenty of light. Young plants do better than old, so a good supply of new cuttings should be taken from vigorous spring or mid-summer plants.

Hibiscus rosa-sinensis

Chinese Rose
Chinese Hibiscus
Shoe Flower

The breath-taking splendour of the *Hibiscus* flower makes this plant one of the greatest delights to the indoor plant lover. Each bloom may last for only one day but if carefully tended the plant will flower abundantly throughout a long season. Hibiscus needs as much sun and light as possible with liberal watering and good drainage. A temperature of 15–20°C (59–77°F) is best. The plant may be allowed to dry out and lose its leaves during winter or it may be kept watered, so retaining its leaves. The only drawback to this plant is its proneness to green fly. Keep some insecticide handy.

Hippeastrum

Amaryllis
Barbados Lily
Mexican Lily

The Amaryllis has large, striking trumpet-shaped flowers and is a favourite perennial pot plant, ideal for indoor cultivation. It may be planted at any time of the year (although usually in spring) and does not seem to mind the dryness caused by central-heating. The bulb should be planted so that half is above soil, well watered and then kept almost dry until the bud starts to grow. After flowering they need plenty of water and maximum light. Allow the plant to dry out in autumn and keep in a warm dark room until growth begins again. It should be re-potted every two years after flowering.

Hoya carnosa

Wax Flower

This plant produces bunches of waxy flowers from early summer to early winter. A rampant climber, it can be trained into various arched shapes and is decorative at all times of the year because of its foliage. Water well during the growing season but reduce the supply in winter. It likes plenty of light. Propagate by cuttings.
Above and left

Hyacinthus See Bulbs

Hyacinth

Hydrangea

The *Hydrangea* is a popular spring-flowering plant, producing spectacular blooms in white, pink, red and blue. Cool, light conditions are required and when in growth they must have plenty of water. Dry air and draughts can be fatal. After flowering is over put the plant in a cool, frost-free place until growth buds appear again. Blue *Hydrangeas* need an acid soil and if you wish to maintain the colour add a teaspoonful of alum to a gallon of water at each watering, or mix aluminium with the potting soil.

Hymenocallis speciosa

Spider Lily
Lily Basket
Peruvian Daffodil

This evergreen plant has unusual fragrant white flowers in the form of graceful shoots radiating out from a central cup. The bulb should be planted with its neck above the surface of the soil in a pot large enough for root growth. It needs a moist soil and a warm temperature throughout the year with plenty of light.

Impatiens

Busy Lizzie
Patience Plant
Patient Lucy
Touch-me-not
Balsam
Water Fuchsia

This is possibly the most popular of all flowering pot plants, easily grown from seed or cuttings. The flowers come in shades of red, salmon and cream to white and it is possible to keep the plant flowering continually all winter. Water copiously when flowering and keep it in a position away from direct sun. Exposure to draughts or too dry an atmosphere will cause the lower leaves to drop off.
Top right

Iris See Bulbs

Jacobinia magnifica

This makes a very fine window plant as it needs a good deal of light to flourish. Elongated, tubular pink blossoms will be produced in the summer and should be watered well. When the flowers have faded the plant needs to be pruned or it will become unshapely. It is particularly prone to red spider mite.

Jasminum officinale

Jasmine

This is a lovely indoor plant with its graceful foliage and the intoxicating scent of its pure white flowers. Unfortunately it does not take kindly to being grown indoors and for this reason is never a particularly long-lasting plant. It needs full light with moisture, a high degree of humidity and a moderate temperature. If you do manage to maintain these conditions, cut the plant back after flowering, place in a sunny position, water well and with luck you get new buds starting up. *Far left*

Kalanchoe blossfeldiana

Vulcan   Good Luck Plant

This succulent plant has compact clusters of small scarlet flowers which bloom in mid-winter. It can be purchased then or grown from seed a little later. It needs warmth and a moist soil. After flowering cut back the plant and keep it in an open window by the sun and water it regularly. Limit watering in winter so that the soil is only moderately damp.

Lilium candidum

Madonna Lily

This lovely white lily with its fragrant scent makes a spectacular flowering plant. The bulb should be planted shallowly with no more than 2.5 centimetres (1 inch) of compost over the bulb. The soil should be given an initial good soak and then left with little water until growth begins, when it needs plenty of water. Drainage must be good. The foliage needs lots of sun although the temperature should not go beyond 20°C (68°F).

Narcissus See **Bulbs**

Daffodil   Jonquil

Nerine sarniensis

Guernsey Lily

Bulbs for this plant are potted in late summer and strikingly beautiful flowers of rose-pink or scarlet will appear in early or mid-winter. Soil should cover only half the bulb and after its initial watering it should be left in a light place with a temperature of 10–15°C (50–59°F) until the shoots appear. After this the soil must be kept moist but well drained. In summer stop watering the plant and allow it to dry out. Keep the bulbs in a dry, airy place until time for new growth. Do not re-pot for at least two seasons.

Nertera granadensis

Bead Plant   Coral-Bead Plant

A curious-looking but attractive plant with a multitude of bright orange berries lasting well into winter. It is best grown in half-pots because it is very low-growing. It does not mind shade but demands abundant watering when active. Any fragment of the plant with roots will prosper when re-potted.

Passiflora

Passion Flower

A truly rampant climber which must be cut back drastically to be practical as an indoor plant. The flowers are quite unique and the common name comes from the cross-shapes in their centres. (Early Christian missionaries to South America used the flowers to illustrate the story of the Crucifixion.) Growth can be checked somewhat with a resultant increase in flowering if you confine the roots to a small pot. It needs plenty of light and warmth along with a moist soil. If attacked by mealy bugs it should be treated immediately as they can cause great damage.
Right

Pelargonium

Geranium

Geraniums will flower almost continuously throughout the year with no marked period of dormancy. Although red is the usual colour for the flowers you may find pink, orange, scarlet and crimson to magenta. They are easy plants to grow, needing little water, (they can in fact stand long periods of dryness), an average temperature of 15°C (59°F) and plenty of light. Cuttings will take root easily. Watch for white fly and aphis.

36

Primula

Primrose

Primulas are best grown from seed and treated as annuals. Seeds sewn in May will flower in the following late winter. They come in a variety of colours and are a fresh-looking reminder of the coming spring. They like a cool spot in the house and require plenty of moisture although not much light. One warning: *Primulas* can cause an irritating rash in some people who touch them and are sometimes referred to as Poison Primroses.

Rhododendron

Azalea

The rhododendron with its shiny green leaves and lovely flowers makes a fine houseplant. It is an immense genus and many species are suitable for indoor cultivation, but most flourish naturally in the reverse of household conditions so some care is required. They need a light, cool atmosphere, and the soil must be kept moist though well drained. They cannot survive in a hot, dry atmosphere. When the plants develop buds just before the main flowering, any side shoots should be nipped off. Young plants need re-potting annually after flowering is finished, established plants only after several years.
Bottom right

Rochea coccinea

This is a succulent plant which produces clusters of scented, crimson flowers. Mature specimens may grow up to 40 centimetres (16 inches) in height like a small bush. It needs very little water in winter but when buds begin to form it is necessary to increase watering. Keep it in a cool, bright position in the house. After flowering cut back the stems to about 15 centimetres (6 inches) to encourage side shoots.

37

Saintpaulia ionantha

African Violet

Because of its exquisite flowers and velvety leaves the African Violet is one of the most popular house plants—in spite of the difficult conditions it requires. Although you can keep a healthy shop-bought plant in bloom for some two months it requires attention if it is to flower again. It comes from a tropical region and therefore likes humidity and warmth but not direct sunshine which can damage its leaves and flowers. It is wise to keep the plant immersed in damp peat or in a bowl on a layer of pebbles with water up to the bottom of the pot. Even a well-tended African Violet is prone to rot and you should be careful to remove dead leaves and flowers. Leaf cuttings will take root in water.
Below

Schizanthus pinnatus

Poor Man's Orchid
Butterfly Flower

This is a showy plant which will flower profusely from late winter to spring. Seeds need to be sewn in late summer for this magnificent spring display. Potting on is very important as the seedlings grow or the plant may flower prematurely as soon as the root tips touch the side of the pot. Frequent pinching out of the growing tips will encourage bushiness, but no further stopping should be done after late winter. Keep the plant slightly shaded when flowering, and water generously. The plant may need supporting with a cane. They prefer quite a low temperature (10–15°C/50–59°F).

Schlumbergera truncata (syn. Zygocactus truncatus)

Christmas Cactus
Crab Cactus
Lobster Cactus

The Christmas Cactus makes a good hanging plant with its unusual-looking pendulous green branches and pink trumpet-shaped flowers. It needs an open-textured potting soil and excellent drainage. Plenty of light and moisture are necessary when the plant is flowering (at Christmas time in the northern hemisphere as the common name suggests) and thereafter it should be kept dry and cool and in a light, airy position until new buds appear.
Left

Sinningia speciosa

Gloxinia

Gloxinia have velvety green leaves and produce grand, trumpet-shaped flowers in late summer and early autumn. It is one of the easiest

summer flowering plants to care for and one of the most colourful. When in full growth it will need plenty of water and good light. The leaves are brittle and mark easily so try to avoid watering directly on to them. When flowering has finished allow the plant to dry out and save the tubers. Start them up the following spring by half burying them in peat. Re-pot when they have developed a number of new leaves.
Right

Solanum capsicastrum

Christmas Cherry
Winter Cherry

The Christmas Cherry is a small shrubby plant which bears shiny red balls of fruit. (These berries are poisonous and must be kept away from children.) In winter this plant begins to appear in shops and you should be careful to pick one with a large number of green cherries. It will not survive in heavy shade or excessive heat, either of which will almost inevitably result in loss of leaves and berries. Put the plant in a light but not directly sunny position and keep the soil moist. It is an annual and should be thrown away when the berries have dropped off.
Bottom right

Sprekelia formosissima

Jacobean Lily

A long stalk bears the graceful orchid-like flower—either crimson or white—of the Jacobean Lily. To achieve flowering the bulb should be only partially covered with soil in a pot allowing good drainage. After an initial soaking it should be kept on the dry side until there are signs of growth. Then it needs plenty of water until it has flowered and the leaves begin to die. Rest in winter and restart in the spring for summer flowers. It needs plenty of light and a warm temperature.

Stephanotis floribunda

Clustered Wax Flower
Madagascar Chaplet Flower
Madagascar Jasmine

Stephanotis is especially cherished for the scent of its flowers and is thus considered to be worth the risk of bringing it into the house. A warm temperature is needed (daytime 20–25°C/68–77°F); light and above all moist conditions must prevail or a full-budded plant may gradually yellow and shrivel up. Once established the plant with its glossy green leaves and white waxy flowers is a rampant climber and will need fairly drastic pruning after flowering. Keep a sharp eye out for signs of mealy bug.

Strelitzia reginae

Bird of Paradise
Bird's Tongue Flower
Crane Flower

The flamboyant bird of Paradise flower reveals a galaxy of vivid colours from brilliant orange to blue, but in spite of its exotic appearance it will grow well in less than ideal conditions. Given good light, reasonable warmth, humidity and moisture it will grow rapidly. It will not flower until it is mature but the leaves shaped like those of a banana plant are themselves attractive. It must be kept on the dry side in winter, and as the base grows quickly re-potting should be carried out every two years (in spring before growth re-starts).
Above

40

Streptocarpus hybridus

Constant Nymph
Cape Primrose

This is an easy and rewarding plant bearing clear, soft-blue, trumpet-shaped flowers which can be encouraged to remain for several months. The plant can be raised by seed sown any time from late winter to spring or by leaf cuttings which are taken easily from existing plants. It will need plenty of light, warmth and a moist soil. The plant tends to die back in winter (when you should water less) but soon new leaves will start to sprout.

Thunbergia alata

Black-eyed Susan

Black-eyed Susan is a climbing annual hardy enough to grow outside. However, if you have the room it makes a very attractive indoor plant bearing orange yellow flowers with dark purple centres which are colourful for much of the year. It needs plenty of light, moisture and a warm temperature.

Tibouchina semidecandra

Glory Bush

This indoor shrub produces beautiful, large deep-purple flowers with a velvety sheen. It will flourish indoors in warm conditions if given enough light and kept moist. As it is a naturally large shrub it may become leggy and lose its bottom leaves, but after flowering it can be heavily pruned down. Cuttings of half-ripe shoots can be taken at any time to produce new plants.

Tulip See **Bulbs**

Vallota speciosa

Scarborough Lily

Plant this bulb sometime between spring and mid-summer and it will produce brilliant scarlet flowers by late summer or early autumn. Pot so that the soil covers half the bulb, water well and place in a bright position. Do not water again until sprouts appear and then keep the soil constantly moist. After flowering leave the bulbs in a dry, airy place until it is time to re-start them. They only need re-potting every two to three years.
Bottom right

Vriesia splendens

Flaming Sword

The bright red sword-shaped bracts of the *Vriesia splendens* will last for some eight weeks although its yellow flowers are short-lived. Keep the plant away from strong sunlight in a warm position, watering freely in summer into the rosette of leaves as well as into the soil. Cut down watering in winter. After flowering prune back the old leaves to make way for new growth. The plant is unlikely to flower again, but the foliage is very attractive on its own.
Top right

Zantedeschia aethiopica

Arum Lily   *Lily of the Nile*
Trumpet Lily   *Calla Lily*

The long stalks of the Arum Lily carry snowy white flowers with an intoxicating scent. The surrounding leaves are like smooth green arrows. Bulbs should be planted in early autumn about 2.5 centimetres (1 inch) below the soil, given a good soaking and then watered sparingly until sprouts appear. Then more liberally. Watering from below reduces the possibility of rot at the base of the leaves. Place in a warm, light position.
Left

2 Foliage Plants

Asparagus sprengeri

Asparagus Fern
Emerald-feather Fern

This so-called "fern" (actually a member of the lily family) can be grown and trimmed to cascade attractively over a bowl or basket. It is a decorative and undemanding plant growing well in a shady situation and requiring a moist though not wet soil.
Top left

Aspidistra eliator

Bar-room Plant
Cast-iron Plant

This hardy foliage plant—an old English favourite in Victorian times—tolerates extremes of temperature and poor lighting, disliking as it does strong sun and over-watering. It responds to care by giving shiny dark leaves which should be cleaned occasionally with a mixture of milk and water. Do not keep in too large a pot; it flourishes best when pot-bound.
Bottom left

Begonia rex

Merry Christmas
Fairy Plant
Fan Plant

The colourful, patterned leaves of the *begonia rex* make it an outstanding foliage plant. It needs a moderate temperature and constant humidity (being intolerant of dry air) and copious watering during the growth season. However, it has a dormant period in the winter when it should be allowed almost to dry out. Mildew can be a problem in the damp conditions necessary for growth and it may become leggy after a year or two. Fortunately it is easy to propagate by leaf cuttings.
Opposite

Caladium candidum

Angel's Wings

This plant is valued for its decorative foliage—heart-shaped, white leaves with dark green veins. A plant that is bought in leaf in spring should be kept moist and warm (20°C/68°F) with high humidity for best results. This is never more than a temporary houseplant, however, and the foliage will die down in middle to late summer. After this, keep the tubers dry and warm until early the following spring, when they should be started into growth in moist peat at about 21°C (70°F). Pot into a peaty mix.

Calathea zebrina

Zebra Plant

If given proper attention this can be a truly spectacular plant with light and dark emerald-green leaves that have a velvet sheen. It is particularly suitable for warm, humid conditions. However, with care this atmosphere can be created around a pot plant which is kept out of draughts, watered well and kept reasonably humid, perhaps with a bowl of water next to the plant. It should be re-potted annually (from summer to spring) and can be propagated by division at the same time.

Chlorophytum comosum

Spider Plant
Spider Lily
St Bernard's Lily
Wandering Jew

The Spider Plant has long, arching green leaves with a creamy central stripe, and the mature plant produces young, perfectly formed plantlets on the ends of stalks which give the appearance of spiders hanging from a web. These plantlets are a ready-made source of propagating material needing only to be pegged down into small pots filled with compost. Adequate water should be given from early spring to autumn, slightly less in winter. Keep it in good light.

Cissus antartica

Kangaroo Vine

The attraction of the Kangaroo Vine is its glossy green leaves, oval in shape with serrated edges. It is a natural climber or can be used in a hanging basket and makes a very tolerant houseplant as it will stand cool temperatures and not very much light. Keep well watered during the summer and just moist in winter.
Bottom left

Coleus blumei

Salmon Lace
Flame Nettle

An impressive foliage plant with its richly coloured leaves, *Coleus blumei* grows readily indoors. It is usually kept for one season only but can be easily propagated from cuttings. To keep the plant bushy new buds must be pinched out. It is prone to mealy bug and green fly. Keep the plant in a warm environment with the soil reasonably moist.

Collinia elegans (syn. **Neanthe elegans**, **Chamaedorea elegans**, **Chamaedorea pulchella**)

Palm

Originally from Mexico this plant is one of the easiest dwarf palms to grow, reaching a height of about 45 centimetres (18 inches). It does not mind a dry atmosphere needing less moisture and feeding than most, and is highly resistant to pests and diseases. The best method of propagation is by seed.

Cryptanthus bromelioides tricolor

Earth Star

Cream and green leaves suffused with pink make this a beautiful display plant resembling a starfish in shape. Unlike most bromeliads, the Earth Star does not produce a very interesting flower and is therefore valued mainly for its extraordinary foliage. It needs warm, light conditions and the winter temperature should not fall much below 13°C (58°F). It should be kept on the moist side in summer and on the dry side in winter.
Above

Cyperus alternifolius

Umbrella Plant

This plant is so-called because of its green clusters of umbrella shaped leaves. It is an easy and attractive plant which sprouts to a height of about 60 centimetres (2 feet) when the roots are confined to pots. It needs plenty of water and is best left standing in a dish of water. It has the advantage of not requiring much light. A temperature between 15–20°C (59–68°F) is best.

49

Dieffenbachia

Dumb Cane

This plant has attractively marked leaves and makes an elegant contribution to a group of foliage plants. The odd common name comes from the effect of its poisonous sap. If it touches your mouth your tongue swells up rendering you speechless, so it is well to keep this plant away from children. It needs a warm humid atmosphere and a minimum winter temperature of 15–20°C (59–68°F).

Dizygotheca elegantissima (syn. Aralia elegantissima)

False Aralia   Finger Aralia

This plant has delicate, feathery leaves that are rather like those of a fern. Although a slow grower, it can develop to a considerable size and new buds should be pinched out to check upward growth. Shaded, moist, draught-free conditions suit it best with the temperature not going below 15°C (59°F).
Bottom left

Euphorbia pulcherrima

Poinsettia

The poinsettia with its spectacular brilliant red bracts deserves its immense popularity as a Christmas plant. Choose a sturdy plant with leaves a rich green and no sign of wilting. You will have a longer lasting plant if the tiny flowers at the centre of the bracts are only just coming out. A poinsettia needs good light, moist soil and a constant temperature of 16°C (61°F). If you wish to keep the plant once its leaves are gone, cut down the stems to 10–12 centimetres (4–5 inches) and keep it dry and warm until new growth appears when it is best to pot on. To flower, allow no artificial light in the evening from early autumn.
Right

Ficus elastica

Indiarubber Plant
Rubber Plant

The Rubber Plant is very popular both for its smooth, large oblong leaves and its ease of handling. It is a tough plant which, contrary to its tropical origins, can do well even in the dry atmosphere of a centrally heated room. Place it in a bright position at a temperature around 20°C (68°F). In winter it will have a dormant period when it should be kept on the dry side until new shoots start again. If the youngest leaves are small and wrinkled it may need re-potting although in general it won't mind being severely pot-bound. Its leaves should be sponged with a solution of milk and water.

Grevillea robusta

Silk Oak   Silk Bark Oak

The Silk Oak with its delicate, feathery leaves fares best in cool, light conditions. It will develop into a plant of considerable size if the growing tips are not removed at an early stage in order to create outward growth. Never allow the soil to dry out completely, and regular feeding of an established plant is a must.
Bottom left

Gymura aurantiaca

Velvet Plant

This vigorous climbing plant is covered with tiny hairs which give a velvety look to the leaves in the right light. Although it produces small orange flowers they unfortunately have a disagreeable odour and must be pinched out. Leaf growth must also be pinched out if you want to maintain a compact plant or you can train it around a support. It should be kept on the dry side in moderately cool conditions with plenty of light.

Hedera

Ivy

Ivies are among the easiest, least demanding house plants and are very popular because of this. They do best in cool positions reasonably well lit and not too damp. Most can be used as climbers or trailers. To aid appearance the leaves should be sponged frequently. Cuttings will root easily.

Above

Helxine Soleirolii

Mind-your-own-business
Baby's Tears
Irish Moss

This pretty, green creeping plant is easy to grow, rapidly producing mounds of tiny leaves. An inquisitive finger prodding at the plant will produce a tell-tale hole—hence, "Mind-your-own-business". It likes a lot of water but is not fussy about temperature or light, withstanding both cold and shade.

Hypoestes sanguinolenta

Freckleface

Although this is a flowering plant, it is included in this section because it is mainly valued for its unusual evergreen foliage—leaves spotted with pink as if paint had been spilled on them. In a light room, a warm temperature and moist soil it will flourish. Indeed it is likely to become straggly and needs to be pruned regularly. Shoots will root easily and quickly.

Maranta leuconeura

Prayer Plant
Rabbits' Tracks
Husband-and-wife Plant

The exotic *Maranta* with its strikingly marked oblong leaves abhors exposure to direct sunlight. Otherwise it is a fine indoor plant being tolerant of most other conditions. It needs a lot of water and appreciates humidity, so plunging its pot in damp peat will be beneficial. As one of its common names suggests, its leaves fold together like hands in prayer as darkness descends. It should be re-potted in spring when it can be propagated by dividing the roots.
Top left

Monstera deliciosa

Swiss Cheese Plant
Mexican Breadfruit
Hurricane Plant
Split-leaf Philodendron

This popular plant has large, shiny dark green leaves and makes a striking foliage display. It is fairly slow-growing and although tropical in origin it needs less water and humidity than other tropical foliage. Good drainage is important to prevent water-logging and rotting of the roots. Its aerial roots which appear from the stem must not be removed but encouraged to grow

54

into the pot. It is a tough plant but the leaves may turn yellow from over- or under-watering.
Bottom left

Pandanus veitchii

Screw-pine

A superb individual plant with green and white striped leaves rather like giant pineapple leaves (hence, "pine"). The corkscrew form of the mature tree's trunk accounts for the other half of its common name. Its leaves will grow up to 60 centimetres (2 feet) long and are quite durable. In winter it has a dormant season during which it should be kept on the dry side. During growth, however, it needs a lot of heat and moisture and a fair amount of light.
Top right

Pelargonium

Lemon-scented Geranium

This geranium is grown for its scented leaves which will release a pungent verbena odour when lightly brushed. (Other scented geraniums include rose and mint.) It is exceptionally easy to grow requiring very little water, lots of light and an average temperature of 15°C (59°F). It will flourish if not over-watered and cuttings root easily.

Peperomia argyreia

Football Plant
Watermelon Peperomia

This plant has attractive dark green leaves with silver bands. They grow up to 10 centimetres (4 inches) long and are heart-shaped. It needs good light (but with some protection against direct sunlight), and must be watered carefully allowing the roots to dry out a little between each application.
Bottom right

Persea gratissima

Avocado Pear Plant
Alligator Plant

An Avocado Plant is fun to grow from the stone and if tended well it will develop into a stalky tree with a canopy of green leaves. To germinate your avocado, support the stone, pointed side up, over a glass of water (use toothpicks or a cardboard collar for support). The round side should be just touching the water. Leave it in a warm dimly lit place and keep up the water level until it begins to root. Transfer it to a good sandy potting mixture leaving a little of the stone sticking out of the soil. It will grow rapidly in a warm, sunny position. If you want it to branch, pinch out the top buds when it reaches about 20 centimetres (8 inches) high. Keep the plant out of draughts and water when the potting mixture gets dry.
Top left

Philodendron scandens

Sweetheart Vine

The *Philodendron* is one of the most popular of all houseplants—an attractive climbing foliage plant producing shiny, dark-green, heart-shaped leaves. It likes moderately warm conditions (about 16°C/ 61°F) and a fair amount of moisture and light. It is a hardy plant and a vigorous climber, and pruning is essential if you want it to bush out. Stem cuttings with three joints or top shoots root easily.
Top right

Pilea cadierei

Friendship Plant
Aluminium Plant

The *Pilea* is a tough and usually trouble-free foliage plant with green pointed leaves splashed with silver. It grows easily from cuttings and it is best to start new plants (several to

a pot) once a year or so, throwing away the parent plant. It grows rapidly in favourable conditions and pruning is necessary to keep it tidy. It should be fed regularly, shaded from bright sunlight and given plenty of water in summer although less in winter.
Bottom left

Pittosporum

The foliage of the evergreen *Pittosporum* is much used by florists in arranging displays. However, the delightful fragrance given off by its small flowers during winter gives it added value. It does well in cool, well-lit, airy conditions but it seems capable of enduring quite harsh treatment and recovering.

Platycerium

Staghorn Fern

The main fronds of this fern are 60–90 centimetres (2–3 feet) long, dividing sharply half-way up so that they look like antlers. Other smaller fronds are also formed at the base. It thrives in baskets or shallow pans and is a tough plant able to put up with considerable neglect. It likes warmth but not dryness, and to flourish the roots must be kept moist. The plant welcomes a periodic thorough drenching. Keep it away from direct sun.
Right

Polyscias

Ming Tree

The gnarled branches of the mature Ming Tree are part of the strange attraction of this plant although young plants usually have fairly straight, notched trunks or stems. They come from the islands of the South Pacific and South East Asia and therefore need conditions as similar as possible to the rainy tropics. Keep the plant out of direct sunlight in a warm, humid place and keep the soil moist.

Rhoicissus rhomboidea

Grape Ivy
Natal Vine

An evergreen vine with dark glossy leaves, the Grape Ivy is one of the toughest and least demanding of all foliage pot plants. It is ideal for almost any indoor location: hot or cool, moist or dry. It can be used effectively as a room divider or as a brightener for dark corners which other plants cannot tolerate. Water sparingly in winter and keep modestly moist in spring and summer. Keep its leaves glossy by careful cleaning with a milk-water solution.
Top left

Sansevieria

Mother-in-law's Tongue
Bow-string Hemp

Sansevieria is particularly suited to the dry air of a centrally-heated house and therefore is a very successful indoor foliage plant. Its long, sharp-pointed leaves make it a dramatic addition to a plant group. It needs very little moisture and you must take care only to water it when the plant is really dry. Keep in a bright position.
Top right

Schefflera actinophylla

Umbrella Tree

The Umbrella Tree makes an elegant indoor foliage plant with its graceful, sloping leaves. They are elongated in shape and a dark glossy green. It will grow to quite a size in favourable conditions when it stands out well on its own but as a small plant makes a nice addition to a grouping. It will, however, reach a substantial size quite quickly. It is not a demanding plant but likes a light, moderately warm room and a moist soil.
Left

Syagrus weddeliana (syn. **Cocos weddeliana**)

Dwarf Coconut Palm

This is a graceful dwarf palm with delicate arched foliage. Even when young the feathery leaves make it attractive in a plant grouping. Give it plenty of water and a minimum temperature of 15°C (59°F)—more if possible. It is easily available from florists—a good thing because it is not an easy plant to keep.
Right

Tolmiea menziesii

Pick-a-back Plant
Piggy-back Plant

The common name of this plant describes accurately the way new plantlets are produced and carried on the old leaves. These new growths can be removed and propagated in water or moist soil. The downy leaves are heart-shaped with toothed edges and deep green in colour. It is quite an easy compact plant, tolerating low temperatures and poor light. It should always be kept moist.

Tradescantia fluminensis

Quick Silver
Inch Plant

This makes an attractive hanging plant and is quite easy to care for. It must be trimmed back, however, as it will become unkempt and straggly if left on its own. When plain green, unvariegated leaves appear they must be removed immediately or they may begin to dominate the plant. It is best kept in a light position and fed well. The soil should be moist rather than saturated. If, in spite of pruning the plant begins to lose its shape, the best thing is to start a new plant by taking cuttings which will root easily.

Zebrina pendula

This adaptable household plant is often mistaken for *Tradescantia* but in fact has much fleshier leaves and stems. Like *Tradescantia* it does well in a hanging basket where its leaves can be shown to advantage. They are purple underneath and green on top with a silver stripe. They need very little moisture and not much light, flourishing in all sorts of locations. Cuttings will root easily.

Index